This Notebook Belongs To

Made in the USA
Monee, IL
24 July 2021

74213347R00069